Gypsy Architecture

Gypsy Architecture

Houses of the Roma in Eastern Europe

Texts
Renata Calzi
Patrizio Corno

Photographs
Carlo Gianferro

Edition Axel Menges

Dedicated to Massimo Costa

ISBN 978-3-936681-12-3

Prepress work: Reinhard Truckenmüller, Stuttgart
Printing and binding: Everbest Printing Co., Ltd., China

Translation into English: Neil Stratton, Oxford
Editing: Dorothea Duwe
Jacket design: Axel Menges

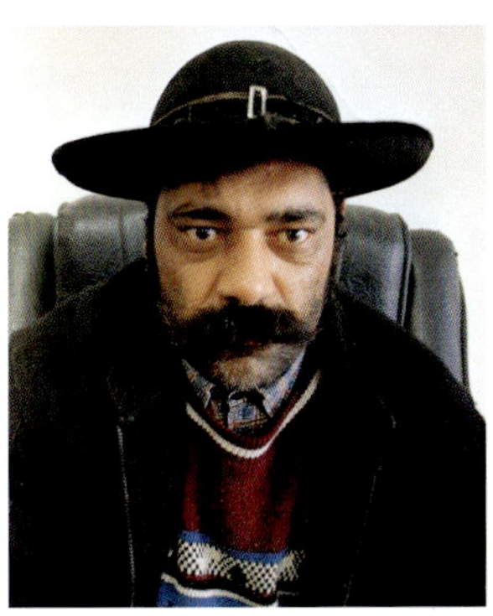

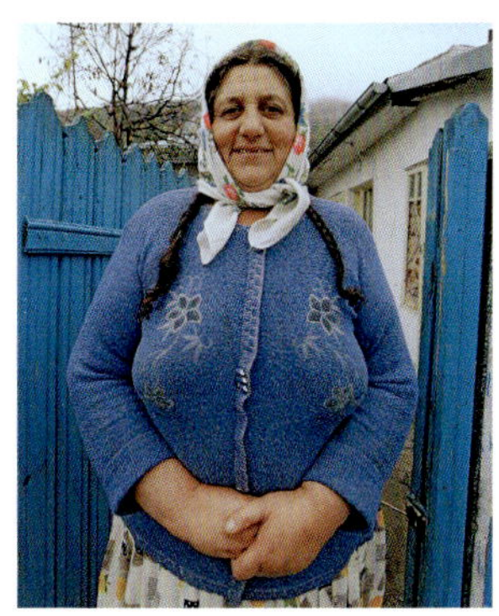

Otaci
Soroca
Rescani
Botosani
Suceava
Moldova
Oradea
Zalau
Bistrita
Iasi
La Ciuria
Chisinau
Piatra Neamt
Roznow
Cluj Napoca
Tirgu
Mures
Bacau
Arad
Miercurea
Cluc
Deva
Timisoara
Sibiu
Ivesti
Liesti
Focsani
Brasov
Galati
Resita
Rimnicu
Vilcea
Romania
Braila
Tulcea
Belgrade
Drobeta-
Turnu Severin
Ploiesti
Strehaia
Slatina
Bucharest
Craiova
Sintesti
Buzescu
Giurgiu
Alexandria
Sofia
Skopje

Preface

Patrizio Corno

The origins of this work, this book, begin, as is often the case with me, in its epilogue.

In fact, without the surprising far-sightedness of Dorothea Duwe, managing editor of Edition Axel Menges, this very long piece of work undertaken by Renata, Carlo and myself would undoubtedly have been destined to return to our archives for a future occasion. Instead, she intuitively understood the value of this piece of research as she quickly ran her eyes over the images of a mock up of *Gypsy Architecture*, produced with the aid of Massimo Costa in his role as a graphic artist; offering, as it does, an immediate, rapid and intriguing view of a new world that is almost unknown in the West – the new, static world of the Gypsies.

That day in Frankfurt other publishers had had a chance to evaluate our work but none had been capable of moving beyond their own, restricted outlook. They all asked us for houses, interiors, architecture, that were now known and firmly established in contemporary culture. They perhaps did not understand or did not want to understand that a book is a means of learning, of spreading knowledge, a mirror in which people search for images of the humanity to which we all belong, but images that are remote and new, different and unusual, and influenced by the geography and by the history of this always green and ever moving apple. Images and iconography that certainly form part of the imagination of our dreams because, being human, we share a common background and each of us is undoubtedly able to mentally tune into the imaginative activity and perception of each person like ourselves whatever their geographical or genetic origin.

As a frequent visitor to Eastern Europe, I have come to know people who are very smart in business, highly perceptive culturally or aesthetically or very aware of the social changes in progress in places that at first sight have seemed to me to be sterile, Soviet relics of a world that was but that does not exist; that is changing sluggishly and with effort but which is able to produce, even though in very small numbers, people whose cultural or business activity owes its origin to the now dominant Western culture.

In Moldova, a country that is almost unknown in Italy and, as far as I am aware, the rest of the world, which was the starting point for this work, people with quite extraordinary perception and practical capabilities live and work.

I have got to know and work for Anatol Stati, whose oil company, which has been in business for no more than twenty years, is now able to stand up to the world's oil giants, anticipating them and beating them to the post, playing one of the few real cards one can today: perceptive ability combined with decisiveness and the absolute willingness to take calculated risks.

I know but, for reasons of time and opportunity, have not spent time with Costantin Tanase, whose far-sighted vision of the present in his articles in *Timpul* is able to create crude and impossible scenarios for the future of this nation of Moldova.

I know Juri Leanca, although unfortunately I have not spent as much with him as I would like. His mildness is actually strength and determination and his vision of the future justifies the hideous current cultural impasse and paves the way for this nation, which will undoubtedly find the determination to emerge in splendour and true to itself in its romantic, rural tranquillity.

I knew, spend time with and will spend time with Robert Cerari. Styled the Viceroy of the Gypsies of Moldova and all the Russias, he is in actual fact a calm and capable businessman who, without betraying his Romany origins, decided, since he preferred the settled life of Soroca to the traditional wandering, to found commercial enterprises, creating both business and work for the indigenous local population.

Besides Robert Cerari, Renata and Carlo have got to know and have spent time with, albeit very briefly, Artur Cerari, Baron of the Gypsies of Moldova and all the Russias; the Bulibasha of Buzescu in Romania, men who are responsible for many people, Viorica the Gypsy activist and Gheorghe the singer of Bicaz in the northern Carpathians, who are the subject of Renata's joyful and fantastic tales that have been gathered together for this publication.

My interpreter, Valerio Anischieschievici from Chisinau, is someone I have known and spent time with for years. Not only has he translated Russian or Romanian for me but above all he has interpreted and made me understand local attitudes and opinions, which were frequently incomprehensible to me or very different from my own.

Then at Frankfurt, at the 2005 Book Fair, Carlo and I met and got to know Dorothea Duwe, whose calm far-sightedness enabled us to talk to Axel Menges, the publisher. He, in a very short space of time, quietly and calmly decided to join us in this new, risky and exciting publishing adventure, which had been begun three years earlier on a bitterly cold winter's day in Soroca, a small town in northern Moldova.

The people I have got to know in this small nation have enabled me to gain a deeper understanding of the new and complex realities of these Eastern European countries that for decades remained unknown to us Western Europeans and persuaded me to tell the tale in the best possible way of the incredible journey that Renata Calzi and Carlo Gianferro had set out and managed to undertake, relying solely on my perception of a situation, an architecture that existed, that was new, unknown, phantasmagorical, very real but certainly »ultra«: Gypsy architecture.

Settled Gypsies?

Patrizio Corno

I accompanied an Italian friend to Soroca, a small, quiet town in the north of the Republic of Moldova on the river Dnieper, which marks the border with the Ukraine. I went partly to help him with what he was looking for and partly to expand my knowledge of this country where I have been working for three years, alternating in my architectural practice between frequent stays in the capital, Chisinau, and Milan in Italy.

The mayor received us and, after having briefly told us about the life of the town and listed the interesting places and buildings to visit, he very kindly, since we were foreigners, also offered us the deputy mayor as a tour guide. The day was dreary, grey and very cold. The trip had started in good time but had become very difficult. The roads, which were already shocking, were now also snow covered, and, despite the fact that the distance from Chisinau was only around 150 km, it had taken us more than four hours.

I was in a very bad mood. Surroundings affect my moods a great deal and sad, grey and crumbling Soviet towns usually have a very negative influence on me. However, despite everything, I intended, as always, to see as many things and people as possible.

The town's tourist attractions consisted of a medieval castle built by Stefan Cel Mare (Stephen the Great), the only Moldovan king who had been able to organize the region militarily and withstand the attacks of the Turkish Empire for more than forty years; and a viewing platform. This terrace was as incredible as improbable and it was still in the process of being built on the top of a hill that took me an immense amount of effort to climb. From the height of the terrace there was a splendid view. The river loops at this point and it is possible to admire the town in all its drabness stretched out along the river in the shelter of the castle. On the descent, the deputy mayor, besides telling us about the very limited hotel accommodation, which we were going to need for the night, also mentioned to me, without making any special point about it – in fact almost reluctantly – that there was also a strange, mysterious quarter situated on a hill on the outskirts, outside the town proper but still a part of it, which it was possible to reach by a road that ran to it but no further.

The quarter, continued the deputy mayor, was recent and had been begun by the Gypsy, Romany or whatever community no more than ten years ago.

Gypsies? thought I, settled Gypsies? I imagined a shanty town built with whatever came to hand, perhaps exploiting the travelling caravans that these people usually use as fixed supports.

My innate curiosity and the desire to avoid future regrets egged me on to visit the place, all the more because at best the town might offer a warm meal on this dreary day.

The road climbed along the side of a hill and as it gradually rose I could not believe what I was seeing from the car window. Alas, I left childhood and the world of fairy stories behind years ago but what slowly appeared as I advanced was a world of dreams and fairy tale.

On either side of the deeply cut up and very dirty road stood fantastic edifices in the literal meaning of the term. Villas with Indian-style roofs, extravagant wrought-iron railings, two storey buildings covered with multi-coloured marbles or variously decorated with a wide range of colours and materials.

One villa, which later turned out to be the home of Artur, the Baron, was enormous. Built on two floors of red brick, it had twisted columns surmounted by an Indian-style sheet metal roof.

Hens and geese scratched around the courtyard before the house and in it were parked two enormous black cars with their wheels buried. These looked vaguely American but had been built in Russia. They explained to me that one had once belonged to Brezhnev and the other to Suslov, members of the Politburo in Moscow, but that they had now been acquired by the Baron as part of his collection and helped to maintain the high prestige of Artur, King of the Gypsies of Moldova and all the Russias.

Another villa, which was still being built, was capped by a full size copy of the quadriga from the Brandenburg Gate in Berlin.

The »Gypsy« quarter crowned the citadel and ironically its position, which had been stipulated by the town council and which was located on the outskirts of the »official« town so as not to disturb the harsh unchanging life of Soroca, had ended up by coming to dominate the scene. The richness, the size of each villa and that of everything together, the great variety of wall ornaments and decorative materials all meant that this was a ghetto with a difference.

Anyone viewing Soroca from this brand new, extremely architecturally rich quarter, would seem to be looking down into the bottom of the valley on a town of the poor, of helpless people in a constant struggle with the difficulties of everyday life, a desolate grey land made up of uniform Soviet era apartment blocks that stood for all that the Soviet Union had been and was.

I spent several hours in the quarter and I managed to be received by the chief, the Baron as Artur Cerari is styled, who delightedly sought not just to show but to explain the reason for this new – to me – urban reality, for these buildings, these structures that eluded any architectural classification and that belonged to the dream world, to the dream that the Romany people today have of integrating themselves with the local populations. To achieve this end they have adopted the most edgy and individual of images, but also the most striking, violent and vulgar yet visually imaginative, just as in other contexts we do in our habits as we follow the latest trend or trends leading us to think and live total living.

The quarter consists of around fifty villas, each different from the others and all built after 1992, the year in which Moldova, freed from the Soviet Union, began to enjoy freedom and individuals were able to express themselves and grow through their activities.

The Romany or Gypsies, without intending anything by the term beyond a convenient name by which to call them, had already been settled in Soroca for some years, either because it was close to the border or perhaps because social conditions in the town had favoured settlement due to its remoteness from the capital.

The Soroca group was largely made up of Calderai [metalworkers] families and it is likely that the usefulness of their activities and those of other experts in metal forging persuaded the local authorities not just to allow them to settle but even to allow them to use some small crumbling buildings – more shacks than houses – around which the Gypsy community gathered and formed a stable body.

Over time, the families, after having acquired the land, began building, competing with each other to construct the largest, the most striking, the most eye-catching house, because the house, then as now, represents the family, its standing, its power and its wealth.

Uninfluenced by any knowledge of architectural culture, each family head chose the style, size and finishings on the basis of his own personal tastes or memories of travels, houses and things seen in other countries. The result has been the creation of bizarre and fantastic jumbles of buildings that it is hard to classify in terms of western stylistic features. Very often the houses are the result of enormous jigsaw puzzles created from an assembly of images or photographs of various different buildings, and their execution precisely follows these crazy guidelines, perhaps because they are incomprehensible to those carrying out the project.

Otherwise, how could one possibly explain Indian-style roofs crowning neoclassical buildings, mansard roofs on structures of improbable style, Frenchified Chinese pagodas, heterogeneous assemblies of diverse and contrasting elements.

Looking at the photographs taken by Carlo Gianferro, I have to say, amongst other things, that the structures, the villas gradually soften their bizarre and fantastic imagery the closer they are built to European countries. Undoubtedly, the cultural influence of neighbouring countries already immersed in the culture and lifestyle of Europe has helped to »contaminate« the owners and bring their dwellings, the expression of their wishes, more into line with the ruling culture.

What, however, remains staggering is the quality of the execution of the complex decorations, of the architectural elements and buildings that are very often contrasting, of widely differing façades surmounted by steepling roofs of no practical use whose only function is to represent, through their lack of proportion and absolute needlessness, the financial and social power of the family. Besides pieces of sculpture that are undoubtedly ritual and symbolic and originating from Indian culture, suns with spiny rays, various forms of pinnacle, geometrical moons, zoomorphic decorations, the tops of the roofs bear metalwork inscriptions giving the date of building and the name of the family or that of the wife, symbolizing a desire for display and the proclamation of ownership. Their observation alone would merit a specific study.

The visit to the Gypsy quarter of Soroca triggered my desire to know, to see and to understand. However, the usual urgent and pressing professional commitments prevented me.

I passed on my interest to Renata Calzi and Carlo Gianferro, who, after an initial visit and report from Soroca, decided to continue the journey and entered into a fantastic world unknown in the West. It is the story of this that is told here through the brief accounts by Renata of their experiences and the images captured by Carlo with his sensitive and professional eye.

Gypsy architecture

Renata Calzi

I am on the tube.

I am seated and I look around. The carriage is full of people, tired, cross people. Most are listlessly reading the newspaper, others follow their own thoughts gazing into space. Yet others chatter to each other. The atmosphere of the carriage is heavy with weariness and apathy. Braking shakes me from my thoughts. The carriage doors open. People leave and people enter. The doors squeal as they close. The tube moves off again.

»Good morning ladies and gentlemen. Good morning everyone. Now I will play something for you. Thank you ladies and gentlemen …«

The notes of the instrument swell in the air. I turn my eyes searching for their point of origin. I follow them, almost visually, as the sound pursues its path between the bodies of a score of people. The source is a man, whose nimble hands touch and brush a violin.

The man is scruffy, the clothes are threadbare and of different sizes but they are not dirty. Only on his face are there traces of sweat. It is slightly dirty and the complexion of the face is olive. His hair is dark and his black eyes have a vaguely oriental slant.

The figure with the violin stands out amidst the mass of grey suits of the other passengers, who remain motionless, as if paralysed and frozen in the same positions.

The notes continue to twist and turn between the floor and ceiling of the carriage …

He is a Gypsy, like so many of those who play for this underground railway community.

A paper Coca-Cola cup comes out of his jacket pocket. Folded. Coins and change jangle within it.

»Thank you ladies and gentlemen. Thank you very much. I ask you for a little help. Thank you.«

I close my eyes and I imagine a Gypsy in another place. I imagine him as he plays by his colourful caravan, in the midst of others, in a travelling camp on the outskirts of a town. He plays by the fire. He plays for his friends and family, who beat the rhythm of the song with their hands. His wife wears a coloured petticoat, whilst the barefooted children play amongst the ruts in the ground caused by the heavy and luxurious towing vehicles. The camp I imagine is like any other in the world. A modern day clone of the eternal encampments of a people without a state who live by moving from country to country, foreigners in every homeland.

Eternally stateless, occasional guests of the countries they encounter on their path.

This is how I imagine them. This is how I see them. I catch myself thinking, »where do they come from?«

From the East. From Spain. These are the most obvious answers. Our imagination places them in these territories. To a degree it is true. Most come from these areas but their origins are more distant, in another continent. Asia, India to be precise. This is their land of origin.

Around the year one thousand, maybe earlier, fleeing from conflicts with neighbouring tribes or perhaps to avoid prolonged famines, they set off on their travels. The real reasons and date for the exodus, the diaspora of this people remains a historical mystery. Their traditions, on the other hand, are real. Skilled metalworkers because of their passion for horses, wonderfully talented musicians and fine dancers.

These attributes have enabled them to earn a living amongst the peoples they have encountered during their long pilgrimage in search of a new, never found, never defined homeland.

Some travelled from Persia and the Middle East as far as Morocco, across the Straits of Gibraltar and into Spain. Other crossed the Balkans and in this general area tens of millions of Romany currently live.

They are primarily to be found in Romania, scattered over the Carpathians, the forests of Transylvania and the Moldovan plains as far as the mouth of the Danube. Many live on the edge, in the most absolute poverty. Other more fortunate ones, or rather ones who have been better able to interpret and interact with the new frontiers of capitalism, have come to a halt, settled down and built new villages, constructing what is virtually a new homeland.

I open my eyes again. I no longer imagine Gypsies camped on useless land with their large and often battered caravans. Now I place them in towns, villages or quarters. I place them in a house. Their house.

Following this vision, this curiosity triggered a desire in me to produce a book/report telling the story of their world and illustrating their structures, which I do not know but which might be beautiful, interesting and unusual.

I travelled throughout Romania and the Republic of Moldova, interviewing many people to understand the »hows and whys« of the unknown and highly individual explosion of building that I uncovered.

Carlo Gianferro took the photographs that record the houses, people, places and situations.

We met Romany living in large villas that featured unusual and imaginative architectural styles. We visited houses, villas packed with references gathered by the owners on their travels around the world, transported down to the last detail and recreated amidst the brick walls, the

Model of the palace of the emperor of the Gypsies in Sibiu, Romania.

white marbles, the finely worked and traceried, galvanized metal pagoda-style roofs, masterfully handled wrought-iron gates, metal castings transformed into life size statutes of horses, eagles, lions and neoclassical putti, bas reliefs and twisted columns. A new world. A free architecture that is overflowing but unrestrained by the usual codified stylistic features.

We saw and discovered a broad and comprehensive »catalogue« of architecture, but one that was extremely muddled and extraordinary in its new whole. We got to know Gypsies dressed completely in black with flashing smiles of glittering 24 carat gold teeth who sped along crumbling tracks of beaten earth in powerful and luxurious German cars. We met Gypsy wives with plaited hair covered in gold coins and feathers wearing traditional long coloured dresses accompanied by clouds of often dirty, ragged and poorly clothed children, whilst they chattered outside the large villas and warmed themselves beside a fire that had just been lit, and even prepared the dinner in the large cauldrons made by their husbands.

As we toured their quarters and towns we found that it was hard to adapt their travelling tradition to a settled daily life. They still live anchored to a past in the open air that finds it difficult to transform itself and confine itself to the closed rhythms of a room. They possess large buildings, villas, castles with many rooms, but most of the time they live outside, in the street, and often, at certain periods of the year, travelling around Europe to work and make money.

The houses, villas and castles are built in a sort of competition with the neighbours, with other members of the tribe. It seems that, overshadowing the personal pleasure of living in a beautiful home, it is much more important for the Romany to express power and wealth through the use of brick to glorify the image of their family through sheer size. It doesn't matter if only two or three of the score or so rooms in the house are used. It doesn't matter if the children sleep in the drawing or living room in huge double beds. It doesn't matter if at least three different and, naturally, flashy decorative styles clash in the same space. The important thing is to make the neighbours green with envy and to make clear through cubic metres that you are a financially sound person who is flush with cash, and who can take the capitalist world on because you possess all its symbols.

The houses, villas and castles are not designed by famous professionals but by the owners themselves, who have turned themselves into inspired architects and, at times, into lethal engineers, since the dwellings are often twisted by the uncalculated stresses and lean to one side like the Tower of Pisa.

The Gypsies, the Romany, do not even abandon their megalomania when leaving this world. Here too they run to excess, building themselves unusual and magnificent tombs for their eternal sleep. After all, for that world the tomb is a house, a place for eternal rest. We have recorded how the art of the »Calderai« [metalworkers] Gypsies is expressed in their houses. The skill in working metals is amply expressed in the finely embossed, galvanized sheeting of the roofs, in the virtuoso scrolls of the railings surrounding their dwellings. They do not always execute the creations themselves but they are the designers and the result reflects a past that will never disappear from the Gypsy DNA.

These few lines are a summary of what we were able to see and learn of this people who have now almost settled down. The full description of the places, the facts, the people unfolds like a fantastic tale, an underground journey with a stop for each place.

My amazement, my curiosity, the fantastic memory that I have of our travels amongst the Gypsies, the Romany, is that of having discovered, even in social situations that are in many cases debased, the tranquillity, the serenity and the joy of living of this people.

Talking about these situations in a clinical way did not seem to me to be the best way to capture their spirit of life and of describing their amazing constructions.

Rather, the right approach seems to me to be to write in the same way as the Gypsies or Romany pass on their history and their traditions to future generations: illustrating the events like a life story, often adorned with verbal embroidery like the sparkling surfaces of their roofs.

Gypsy Architecture is a cultural trail that does not explain but illustrates how architecture, by its nature one of the most static of arts, has been taken as a frame of reference through which to provide the world with images of the dreams of a people who have wandered throughout the world.

View of Soroca, Gypsy town in northern Moldova.

View of Soroca, Moldova.

House with the horses from the Brandenburg Gate in Soroca, Moldova.

pp. 16/17
Woman seated in front of her home in a Gypsy quarter of Ivesti, Romania.

Details of an embossed zinc-plated roof in Ivesti, Romania.

Detail of a roof and an arcaded wooden loggia in Ivesti, Romania.

Houses with coloured, sheet metal roofs in Otaci, Moldova.

Gypsy woman in front her unfinished house in northern Moldova.
The Gypsies began to build their houses after the fall of the Soviet Union, and the work is still not finished. Many Gypsy quarters or towns are open-air building sites.

pp. 22/23
House with pagoda-style roof in stamped sheet metal.

Children on the majestic flight of marble steps in La Ciuria, Romania.

Wrought-iron gate in Soroca, Moldova. The Gypsies are skilled iron workers. This age-old tradition is handed down from father to son amongst the Calderari, who are fine craftsmen and blacksmiths.

Tulle and bead door used as a divider between rooms in La Ciuria, Romania.

Multicoloured and picturesque entrance in La Ciuria, Romania. Strange furniture delights Gypsies. All the house interiors are colourful.

Interior of the house of Bulibasha Stanescu (head of the Gypsy community) of the Gypsy town of La Ciuria, Romania.

Staircase in the house of Bulibasha Stanescu.

Interior of a house belonging to Bulibasha Stanescu. Guest bedroom.

Portrait of Bulibasha Stanescu in the living/dining area.

Panorama of the town of La Ciuria, Romania, from the terrace of the house of Bulibasha Stanescu.

Gypsy houses in Ivesti, Romania.

Detail of the façade of an enormous, castle-like villa in Liesti, Romania, which is occupied by a family of just three. Several families of birds happily occupy the roof.

Small houses with colourful applied decorations in Ivesti, Romania.

Small houses with colourful applied decorations in La Ciuria, Romania.

Details of roofs in La Ciuria, Romania.

The man with the gold tie

Renata Calzi

Wandering around Romania in the run up to Christmas is very pleasant in many ways.

The people that you meet are very kind and fascinating. They happily talk about their lives and these conversations often take place over wonderful tables groaning with delicious pork dishes. Any occasion serves to drink a toast with guests and drinking a fine cognac, at any hour of the day, beside warm maiolica stoves is a pleasure not to be missed.

In order to interview Gypsies and photograph their homes it is essential to obtain a variety of permissions from the local »Bulibashas«, the heads of the communities, and such meetings often end up unforgettably over a freshly killed pig, boiled or roasted, and served amidst raw, tender savoy cabbage.

The Bulibashas are indisputably charismatic figures and even their clothing reflects their strong personalities. Besides wearing the omnipresent items of black clothing, Borsalino hats and gold teeth, they often adorn themselves with striking and extraordinary accessories.

The meeting with the Bulibasha of Buzescu, a place in the south of Romania, has left a clear and sharp impression in my memory.

We met this incredible figure on a grey day, when the morning struggled to roll back the shades of the night and the Gypsy houses lining the road into the Gypsy quarter had lost the sparkling brilliance of their roofs.

Even at a distance of a hundred metres we can see the striking colour of the tie that he is wearing. He is dressed normally, in a grey suit, a snow-white shirt and a coloured, woollen jumper. On his head a black bearskin.

He waits for us on the pavement, beside his enormous houses we approach, our eyes are drawn and remain glued to his tie. It is difficult to concentrate on his face such is the lure of this extravagant accessory. From a distance, the tie appears to be made from a very bright yellow fabric but close to there is a surprising revelation.

The tie that he is wearing is gold – solid gold. It seems to have been made by a skilful tailor and knitted with gold thread. Diamond-shaped panels decorated with words and flowers complete this surprising creation. One of them bears the name of his recently deceased wife. Looking carefully, we spot the watch chain, solid gold of course, disappearing into an inside pocket of the jacket. On his large fingers he wears six striking gold rings; three on each hand. One depicts the face of Jesus Christ. Two others are engraved with the full body of a lion in relief. A ruby surrounded by diamonds and a blue sapphire set amidst small rubies sparkle on the remaining rings. The array of jewels contrasts with the expression on his face.

The Bulibasha listens, talks and looks at you with the same sad and impassive expression. He exudes ostentatious wealth as an expression of the position of power that he occupies within the community, but sadness of the heart for the premature loss of his much loved wife is also apparent.

The saying »Behind every great man there is a great woman« comes to mind.

Outwardly this man is still great but inwardly, bit by bit, he is shrinking.

He is becoming small again.

(Sic transit gloria mundi.)

(Memento, homo, qui pulvis es ed in polvere reverteris.)

Gypsy workshop in Timisoara, Romania.

A Bulibasha (Gypsy chief) in southern Romania displays his solid gold tie. The name of his beloved dead wife is engraved in the diamond-shaped panels.

House in Otaci, Moldova.

Detail of a highly Oriental-style roof in Otaci, Moldova.

Roof decoration in Soroca, Moldova.

Gate in Soroca, Moldova.

Girl and motor in Soroca, Moldova.

Interiors in Craiova, Romania.

Portrait of Bulibasha Stanescu.

Interior in Drobeta Turnu-Severin, Romania.

Interior in Craiova, Romania.

Interior in Craiova, Romania.

Retouched photo of Gypsy bride and groom.

Detail of ceiling decoration.

pp. 66/67
House with snow in Roznov, Romania.

ADINA

p. 58
Roof of a house in Buzescu, Romania.
The tops of the roofs display the names of the owners, relatives or objects dear to the Gypsies.

p. 59
Roof of a house in Buzescu, Romania.
The balls with points represent the sun.

Houses in Buzescu, Romania.

Roof in Buzescu, Romania.

Son of the Bulibasha in Buzescu, Romania.

Detail of a roof in Buzescu, Romania.

Road in Buzescu, Romania.

Houses under construction in Soroca, Moldova.

Married Gypsy wife in Craiova, Romania. Gypsy women must wear a headscarf in public as soon as they are married.

The magician and the feminist

Renata Calzi

Gypsy women are devoted and obedient wives.

Traditionally, they marry young, very young. No sooner do they reach twelve than they are ready for an arranged marriage.

The families meet to discuss the amount of the dowry rather than the feelings of the bride and groom to be and, once the contract has been agreed, the couple appear at the altar to celebrate the wedding.

As you move around regions where Gypsy influence is strong, you frequently come across girls wearing headscarves, a sure sign that they belong to the clan of wives. As well as not being able to choose their beloved, in many cases girls are not allowed to study. Only far-sighted families permit this kind of distraction, the others only pass on and teach the girls the art of home management. To look after their future children, to honour their husbands and to become tremendous cooks to provide the numerous meals required for the friends of their husbands.

Out of hereditary ignorance, few rebel against a life that is already written and mapped out, but recently a few glimmers of change are appearing in this medieval outlook.

Viorica is a combative and determined Gypsy who lives in a town bathed by the water of the mouth of the Danube. She is a woman whose family has allowed her to study and who works passionately in the Gypsy communities to raise awareness of recent changes in society. Above all she is striving to persuade the men to teach their women to read and write, convincing them of the benefits they will be able to enjoy with daughters or wives who can read a recipe. Viorica travels all over Romania and takes part in various foreign congresses and her tireless efforts are much appreciated and respected by all the travellers, including the men. She remains, however, a woman who loves and who wants to be loved by her man.

Whilst we are guests in the home of the local Bulibasha, the mother of the master of the house enters as we are talking to Viorica. A little old lady who finds it difficult to stay on her feet, she looks at us inquisitively and asks us if we need her powerful favours. I ask myself what kind of favours this aged human can possibly grant.

Viorica then tells me a story. It is her story and that of the old traveller.

A tale that interweaves cultural intelligence with the inherited tradition of Gypsy clairvoyance.

I emerge from the telling of this story incredulous but finally understanding the life of this people.

Up until seven months ago Viorica had been the partner of a foreigner who was living in Romania. They lived together happily for eight years until the moment when her man met a young Romanian girl and, abandoning his beloved, threw himself headlong into new arms. Confronted by this situation, Viorica cried and her heart was sad. The tears flowed freely but she did not lose heart. She found the solution to her problems when she remembered an old woman who lived in her town – a powerful magician known throughout Romania and even Europe whose visions and spells are on the lips of everyone, whether or not they have been miraculously cured. She went to see the famous sorceress and told the tale of her love. They discussed the best cure for recovery and the return of the faithless one. Together they agreed to punish the man by cursing him in a very particular way: he will not be able to make love to women other than her.

After a short while Viorica received a telephone call. On the other end of the line a whining man's voice asked for her forgiveness for his misdeeds. He went on to ask if he could come back to live with her as before and if he could make love to her again. He declared that he had left his young lover because he was no longer able to have satisfactory sexual relations. Neither with her nor with any other woman he had known in the meantime.

Viorica smiles. I look at her amazed. I can't believe it and I ask for confirmation. The answer is affirmative. »It's all true.« Then I ask her another question. »How can an intelligent woman believe in such spells?« The answer is telling.

»How can you not believe in a magic that has been handed down for centuries?

When a mother teaches her daughter what she knows and this knowledge passes from generation to generation until it reaches our days?«

This is culture. A distant culture that has journeyed across continents to Romania from India in the east. And that, with the passage of time, has only been improved.

p. 70
Roof in Roznov, Romania.

p. 71
Details of roofs in Soroca, Moldova.

Coloured roof in Rescani, Moldova.

Roof in Soroca, Moldova.

Portrait of a Gypsy girl in Pietra Neamt, Romania.

Corner of Soroca. Moldova.

Houses in Soroca, Moldova.

The community of Artur

Renata Calzi

Artur Cerari is a Baron, the Baron. He is the Baron of the Gypsies of the Republic of Moldova and all the Russias. He is a king. He is an undisputed chief, but very different from his subjects.

By tradition, the travellers elect a chief. From amongst the host of candidates, one is chosen who has considerable abilities as a mediator, intelligence, firmness, awareness and, above all, great calmness, since the Gypsies inherit a »fiery« spirit that flares up over a trifle. All that is needed is a phrase, a word, a glance and in a few seconds the intonation of the voice rises, the olive complexion of the skin becomes inflamed, hands and arms begin to whirl in the air, which becomes tense and heated.

This is why calmness is a precious quality. Becoming a »chief« means smoothing over the daily disputes, small and large, of the numerous family groups. Transmitting one's own calmness to the entire community is a hard task.

Artur's calm physical appearance makes him seem a chief from the outset. Of medium height and solidly built, a face framed by pepper and salt hair and a forked beard with its two points resting on his chest; dark, shrewd, oriental and extremely lively eyes; strong hands with the inevitable and traditional long nail on the little finger, synonymous with power and determination. Polite in manners, calm in speech and, above all, assured in gestures. Attributes he has inherited from his father, along with the title, which appears almost aristocratic.

Artur lives in a large Arab-style house situated in the heart of the Gypsy quarter of Soroca, a small Russian-style town on the far northern edge of the Republic of Moldova, where the river separates it from the neighbouring Ukraine.

Artur manages and controls a community of around 5,000 Gypsy souls occupying large villas that display magnificent and unusual styles of architecture. Houses packed with references gathered by the owners on their travels around the world and transported down to the last detail amidst the brick walls, the white marbles, the finely worked and traceried, galvanized metal pagoda-style roofs, masterfully handled wrought-iron gates, metal castings transformed into life size statutes of horses, eagles, lions and neo-classical putti, bas reliefs and twisted columns. A wide-ranging and comprehensive architectural catalogue but one that is highly confused.

Houses inhabited by Artur's Gypsies.

Travellers dressed entirely in black with flashing smiles of 24 carat gold teeth who speed in powerful and luxurious German cars along the crumbling, beaten earth streets of the town, littered with potholes and puddles.

Travellers in an exclusively Gypsy bar, drinking bottles of brandy or vodka, immersed in games of cards with much shouting, cards that fly through the air like confetti when one of the frequent disputes breaks out.

Gypsy women with plaited hair covered in gold coins and feathers wearing traditional long coloured dresses accompanied by clouds of often dirty, ragged and poorly clothed children, gossiping on street corners as they warm themselves beside a fire that has just been lit or standing by the road as they prepare the dinner in large cauldrons made by their husbands.

Gypsies you come across in the middle of a dirt patch slaughtering fat white geese, watching you with amusement as you watch them, and who immediately invite you to taste the fresh and delicious results in their enormous houses.

As you tour the quarter so you encounter the traditions of travelling people in practices and customs that are finding it hard to adjust to a settled daily life; and a past in the open air that it is difficult to shoehorn into the closed rhythms of a room keeps showing through. They possess large houses but the cooking is done outside almost as if they do not wish to use or sully the new dwellings. Artur tells us that the houses are not always built for personal pleasure but in a sort of competition with the neighbouring house. Power and display in the form of brick to glorify through sheer size the wealth of the family. It doesn't matter if only a handful of the twenty rooms in the house are actually used. The important thing is to make the neighbours green with envy and to make it clear through cubic metres that you are a financially sound person.

The houses are not designed by famous professionals but by the owners themselves, who turn themselves into inspired architects and, sometimes, lethal engineers, since the dwellings are often twisted or lean to one side like the Tower of Pisa.

If, now they are settled, the Gypsies live in spectacular buildings whilst they are alive, so too when they pass on do they strive for excess in the striking tombs that they build for themselves.

In the local Orthodox cemetery their tombs, one beside another, form a continuous and disquieting sequence of engraved black marble slabs bearing the giant-sized features of the deceased.

Some tombs are actual underground rooms furnished down to the last detail. Artur's mummified father sleeps his unending sleep laid out on the old bed. The bedside table stands next to it with the radio and alarm clock and facing him is the television. He sleeps like a great Egyptian Pharaoh. He wanted to surround himself with the objects that were by him during his nights when he was alive. Discretion dictated that I did not ask whether his wife was keeping him company.

As one walks along the cemetery pathways the smiling deceased watch you. Some are on their feet, others seated. In the case of many, only the face is depicted, with, for the men, a hat on the head and, for the women, the ever present headscarf that indicates their marital status. Overall, the impression made by the tombstones is one of serenity and joy.

When alive the Gypsy is a happy man. When dead the impression he makes on you is the same.

The florid interpreter who accompanies us on this journey frequently repeats that,

»I am Anatol, the happy Gypsy... very happy!«

Cerari, emperor of the Gypsies of all the Russias.

p. 80
The gardens of every house in Soroca, Moldova, contain a small fountain for washing one's hands before entering one's home.

p. 81
House in Soroca, Moldova.

1983
ПОСТРОЕН
ЧЕРАРЬ МИРЧА

House in Soroca, Moldova.

Small Bulibasha.

Man and his hams in Strehaia, Romania.

Requiem for a pig

Renata Calzi

Gypsy quarters are often built on the outskirts of Romanian and Moldovan towns. From a distance they resemble Western residential areas, like those built in the nicest and greenest parts of our towns, where splendid villas sit surrounded by carefully tended gardens and elegant railings; where silence rules the day and urban hubbub is banished from the hushed tree-lined avenues.

The two are, however, only similar in certain respects – in their location towards the outskirts, in the riot of greenery in the gardens of the houses and in the absence of shops, particularly food shops.

As in the West, if you want to shop you have to get in the car and head for the small shops on the edge of the town centre. Western-style shopping centres are still completely absent from Romania.

In some cases the mountain comes to Muhammad and traders tour the quarter. These door to door salesmen move slowly along in their vans, stopping every so often and gathering together the local housewives with their long, coloured plaits. Bread, sweets and vegetables emerge from these mobile shops and pass directly into the hands of the shouting and cheerful customers.

However, it is the sale of animals for food that is the most curious and entertaining. Not only are the purchases made in person but the subjects of the transactions are alive, kicking and standing on their own two or four legs.

As you walk along the dirty roads you come across cars towing trailers with cows, pigs or horses poking out. The vendors and the animals are surrounded by crowds made up exclusively of children and men, with the latter ready to agree a price for the purchase. Small animals, on the other hand, travel in the boot of runabouts and, when needed, the boot is opened and out pop the red combs of plump fowls, the white ears of fluffy rabbits and the tail feathers of elegant turkeys. Finally, once a good price has been reached, the large animals are led by a rope round to the rear of the house to await their dispatch, the »Requiem for a pig«.

For the smaller animals the end can be immediate. On the spot. Large knives appear in the hands of the Gypsies ready to slit their throats at the side of the road. Then everything is carried into the in- or outdoor kitchens of the houses in order to prepare the meals of the day.

The dead animals make no great impression when they are already lifeless but when they are killed in this way, on the spot, the visual image makes a violent impression on your mind, which sends a powerful message to your stomach and arouses a strong desire in you to turn away from the sequence of visions buried in your memory.

We often in fact received invitations to dine from our hosts immediately after the various slaughters. And they were immediately accepted. Because the meat – especially the free-range meat – is good to eat, since no strange or GM foodstuffs have been used to fatten the animals as happens in intensive livestock farming.

In the south of Romania, I think I am right that all parts of the animal are used. Even the rope that binds the animal is used to prepare unadulterated sausages that are tasty and delicious, or for objects used in daily care.

Whilst scouring the Romany quarter of the village of Strehaia in pursuit of the local Bulibasha, we recorded the transformation of a pig. From the producer, the pig, to the consumer, the human being.

The local head man gave us a very warm welcome. It was the hour of the daily meal and the intense cold made it impossible to stay outside, so the chatter continued in the house around a table standing by the majolica stove. The family gathered beside us: father, mother, daughter with son, grandparents and a bustling wide-eyed servant.

The women, with a speed and dexterity that is the mark of true housewives, laid the table, carrying in steaming dishes and wine pressed in the house. The master of the house meanwhile tells us of the quiet life that the Gypsies pursue in this corner of Romania, on the borders with Serbia and Bulgaria.

The menu was typically Romanian/Gypsy: pork in every possible way. A succession of courses with the animal appearing in the guise of sausage, rissole, steak and accompanied by tomatoes in oil and vinegar and a savoy cabbage salad.

In almost all the houses that we entered, the pig was the dominant feature of the cookery. But it didn't stop there. It also played a leading role in domestic cleanliness. Its transformation progressed from appetizing meats that were hung and smoked to large and rounded whitish lumps of perfumed soap, as well as small brushes of coarse bristles and even amusing necklaces made from the teeth of what had been eaten.

Nothing remains of the tasty animal. And the pieces of soap presented as a gift by the kind Gypsies will remain on display in the bookshop as a work of art with a difference.

Robert Cerari and the inside of his house.

Marble steps in Otaci, Moldova.

Man at the entrance to his home in Otaci, Moldova.

Interiors in Soroca, Moldova.

Villa in Ivesti, Romania.

Decorative detail on a façade in Ivesti, Romania.

Roofs in Soroca, Moldova.

Decorative detail on a façade in Ivesti, Romania.

House in Ivesti, Romania.

Decorative detail on a façade in Ivesti, Romania.

Detail of a roof in Liesti, Romania.

House in La Ciuria, Romania.

Residence of the emperor of the Romanian Gypsies in Sibiu, Romania.

SB•05BHE
4WD

The family of songsters

Renata Calzi

Gypsy communities are scattered throughout Romania and the north of Moldova.

Unofficial but realistic figures suggest a Gypsy population of around five million out of a total of twenty million Romanian residents. Their small towns or quarters are to be found in all parts of this territory: in the rich industrial region of Timisoara and Arad, along the course of the Danube and around its delta, in the infamous and quite literally gloomy Transylvania, in the rich plains with their crops of cabbages, grain and sugar beet.

Some of these communities cling to the slopes of the Carpathians close to the Moldovan regions, in the district of Pietra Neamt. In these regions the social contrasts between the poor and the rich Gypsy residents are very clear. There are many quarters where marginalized travellers live in pitiful conditions in dilapidated blocks, whilst a few hundred metres away there stand the rich and sumptuous villas of the more fortunate.

Another feature is that there are many examples of individuals abandoning the rigid traditions of the Gypsies, especially amongst the numerous groups of »Musicians« and »Bear tamers« as they adapt to the rapid modernization of Romanian life.

Many, both men and women, are marrying Romanian citizens and causing irritation in more conservative families. The »Calderai« [metalworkers] ethnic group is the most reluctant to change.

However, amidst this whirl of change the typical friendliness and joviality of the Gypsies remain unaltered.

At Pietra Neamt, we met Gheorghe during a packed meeting of Gypsies crowded into a room, where they were busy discussing matters in their musical but incomprehensible language. This charming Gypsy offered himself as tour guide for visits to the quarters of the town.

Over a steaming tea we immediately got on, even if we communicated mainly by gestures, and in the space of a few hours we became great friends. Using our mobile he called his wife and arranged a dinner complete with music and dancing. With courtesy and firmness he also invited us to stay the night at his house.

Gheorghe lives in Bicaz, a village on the slopes of the northern Carpathians. On the outside, his peasant's house looks Romanian. Unlike other Gypsy houses, it lacks the typical decorated metal roof. His wife is not a Gypsy but a florid and cheerful Romanian. Gheorghe is someone who has broken down and leapt over the wall of traditions. He has three children, the two daughters live and work in Italy and one is married to a Romanian. The son lives with them and is a typical Western boy. The only nomadic spirit in this nuclear family is his. And he is very proud of it.

As we climbed up to the village we stopped to buy the food still needed for the dinner. The fish had to be bought. We did, however, not go to a fishmonger but went into a shack on the bank of a river. The fish came straight out of the river and ended up wriggling in a small plastic bag and was carried still alive to the mistress of the house.

The dinner began with a round of glasses filled to the brim with brandy. It was not to be the only one. Before tucking into the steaming polenta, the blood alcohol levels were already high. We were all merry and joyful beside the only stove in the house. The meal was rapidly devoured and at the end, as promised, the dancing and music began.

Gheorghe took up his accordion and began to play and sing for us. The words of the song were invented on the spur of the moment and the main characters of the story were us »fine Italians«.

For the second piece of music the son's keyboard joined in and the duet continued through the tears that slowly rolled down our faces.

The wife meanwhile gazed adoringly at her men and beat out the rhythm with her hands. A real family of songsters.

During the breaks, Gheorghe embraced us. We were his brothers and sisters and, from now on, nothing would divide us from him and the members of his family. He offered us incredible gifts: a mountain cock killed and stuffed by him for Carlo, the photographer, a small electric fire for our interpreter Anatol, »the happy Gypsy«, and a pot for cooking meat for me. In return for this kindness we offered the only thing we had to hand: the mobile to call his daughters in Italy.

Gheorghe and his wife began and continued the telephone calls to the accompaniment of tears and sobs. They greeted, shouted and were moved to joy by the voice of their only grandson.

Lots of telephone calls were to be made up until the moment they accompanied us to beds placed in welcoming but cold rooms, whilst outside white snowflakes began to fall.

It was time to say goodnight. We must never forget that we are brothers and sisters.

We went to sleep covered by layer after layer of duvets and blankets.

The snow woke us in the morning and in the kitchen a breakfast awaited us that was identical to the food consumed the previous evening.

Gheorghe was sad. He went with us in the car together with the unwieldy cock, as far as the fork where our paths were temporarily to part. We bade him farewell whilst he stood on the pavement of the road.

As we drew away we could see large tears on the face of our »brother« running down to the collar of his coat.

Gheorghe is a sentimental, kind Gypsy … Very kind!

Group of Gypsies in Ivesti, Romania.

Details of houses in Sibiu, Romania.

Details of roofs in La Ciuria, Romania.

Inlaid wooden railing in the residence of the emperor of the Gypsies in Sibiu, Romania.

Detail of the roof of the residence of the emperor of the Gypsies in Sibiu, Romania.

HERMANSTADT
SIBIU

Dining area inside the house of the old emperor of the Gypsies in Sibiu, Romania.

The former empress of the Gypsies of Romania.

B 03 WUY

Chicken seller and part of the Gypsy quarter of Sintesti, Romania.

Part of the Gypsy quarter of Sintesti, Romania.

House in Soroca, Moldova.

Detail of a façade in Timisoara, Romania.

Neoclassical villa in Timisoara, Romania.

Detail of a façade in Timisoara, Romania.

377

Woman in Craiova, Romania.

House in Roznov, Romania.

Decorative details on the roofs in Soroca, Moldova.

2

Detail of an entrance canopy in Pietra Neamt, Romania.

Detail of a roof in Roznov, Romania.

Portrait of a Gypsy woman in Rescani, Moldova. She is displaying the Mater certificate awarded during the Second World War to women who had had 10 children.

Internal loggia in a house in La Ciuria, Romania.

Door and details of a villa in Timisoara, Romania.

pp. 126/127
View of the houses in the town of
La Ciuria, Romania.

Small Gypsy houses in Ivesti, Romania.

View of a street in the Gypsy quarter
in Buzescu, Romania.

Façade of a house in the Gypsy quarter
of Buzescu, Romania.

Images of the Gypsy quarter of Buzescu, Romania.

A young girl in the Gypsy quarter of Buzescu, Romania.

A house in La Ciuria, Romania.

pp. 136/137
Roofs of houses in Liesti, Romania.

2001
RIN DOINA
BADEA

Detail of roof in Buzescu, Romania.

Detail of roof in Strehaia, Romania.

Detail of roof in Craiova, Romania.

pp. 140/141
Detail of the roofs in Piatra Neamt, Romania.

A man and his wife in their dining room in Soroca, Moldova.

A woman with her sons in Soroca, Moldova.

Interior in Craiova, Romania.

Still life in a house in Rescani, Moldova.

Interior of a house in Soroca, Moldova.

Detail of a façade of a house in La Ciuria, Romania.

Husband and wife in Craiova, Romania.

Women portrayed in front of their houses in Ivesti, Romania.

Detail of a balcony in Soroca, Moldova.

pp. 152/153
Gypsy cemetery in Soroca, Moldova.

Gypsy tombs in Soroca, Moldova.

ПЛЕШКО
ВЕРА
АНТОНОВНА
1927-1967
АНТОН
ХАРЛАМОВИЧ
1922-1989
В ГОСТЯХ
ПЛЕШКО

Sacred and profane portrait in Drobeta Turnu-Severin, Romania.

CENTRU PRESTĂRI
SERVICII AGRICOLE
VIDRA